Sexual Disorders

THE ENCYCLOPEDIA OF PSYCHOLOGICAL DISORDERS

Senior Consulting Editor Carol C. Nadelson, M.D.
Consulting Editor Claire E. Reinburg

Charles Shields

CHELSEA HOUSE PUBLISHERS
Philadelphia

The ENCYCLOPEDIA OF PSYCHOLOGICAL DISORDERS provides up-to-date information on the history of, causes and effects of, and treatment and therapies for problems affecting the human mind. The titles in this series are not intended to take the place of the professional advice of a psychiatrist or mental health care professional.

Chelsea House Publishers
Editor in Chief: Stephen Reginald
Production Manager: Pamela Loos
Art Director: Sara Davis
Director of Photography: Judy L. Hasday
Managing Editor: James D. Gallagher
Senior Production Editor: J. Christopher Higgins

Staff for SEXUAL DISORDERS
Prepared by P. M. Gordon Associates, Philadelphia
Picture Researcher: P. M. Gordon Associates
Associate Art Director: Takeshi Takahashi
Cover Designer: Emiliano Begnardi

The Chelsea House World Wide Web address is
http://www.chelseahouse.com

First Printing   .

9 8 7 6 5 4 3 2 1

Library of Congress Cataloging-in-Publication Data applied for
ISBN 0-7910-5320-2

CONTENTS

PSYCHOLOGICAL DISORDERS AND THEIR EFFECT

CAROL C. NADELSON, M.D.
PRESIDENT AND CHIEF EXECUTIVE OFFICER,
The American Psychiatric Press

There are a wide range of problems that are considered psychological disorders, including mental and emotional disorders, problems related to alcohol and drug abuse, and some diseases that cause both emotional and physical symptoms. Psychological disorders often begin in early childhood, but during adolescence we see a sharp increase in the number of people affected by these disorders. It has been estimated that about 20 percent of the U.S. population will have some form of mental disorder sometime during their lifetime. Some psychological disorders appear following severe stress or trauma. Others appear to occur more often in some families and may have a genetic or inherited component. Still other disorders do not seem to be connected to any cause we can yet identify. There has been a great deal of attention paid to learning about the causes and treatments of these disorders, and exciting new research has taught us a great deal in the past few decades.

The fact that many new and successful treatments are available makes it especially important that we reject old prejudices and outmoded ideas that consider mental disorders to be untreatable. If psychological problems are identified early, it is possible to prevent serious consequences. We should not keep these problems hidden or feel shame that we or a member of our family has a mental disorder. Some people believe that something they said or did caused a mental disorder. Some people think that these disorders are "only in your head" so that you could "snap out of it" if you made the effort. This type of thinking implies that a treatment is a matter of willpower or motivation. It is a terrible burden for someone who is suffering to be blamed for his or her misery, and often people with psychological disorders are not treated compassionately. We hope that the information in this book will teach you about various mental illnesses.

The problems covered in the volumes in the ENCYCLOPEDIA OF PSYCHOLOGICAL DISORDERS were selected because they are of particular importance to young adults, because they affect them directly or because they affect family and friends. There are individual volumes on reading disorders, attention deficit and disruptive behavior disorders, and dementia—all of these are related to our abilities to learn and integrate information from the world around us. There are books on drug abuse that provide useful information about the effects of these drugs and treatments that are available for those individuals who have drug problems. Some of the books concentrate on one of the most common mental disorders, depression. Others deal with eating disorders, which are dangerous illnesses that affect a large number of young adults, especially women.

Most of the public attention paid to these disorders arises from a particular incident involving a celebrity that awakens us to our own vulnerability to psychological problems. These incidents of celebrities or public figures revealing their own psychological problems can also enable us to think about what we can do to prevent and treat these types of problems.

Sexuality is only one aspect of a full, loving relationship. Sexual desires and expectations change over the course of a lifetime, and health professionals are careful not to call a behavior or attitude abnormal unless it is causing distress to the people involved. Here, an elderly couple celebrate their long life together.

SEXUAL DISORDERS: AN OVERVIEW

When the topic is sexual behavior, what is considered appropriate and what is not? Sexuality is a subject that is fraught with emotion for most of us. Our sexuality is so closely tied to our identity that sometimes we are uncomfortable discussing the topic of sexual disorders. If during our discussion, we recognize one of our own problems, we wonder if that means we are "weird" or abnormal, mentally unbalanced or immoral. We are not always certain which behaviors are appropriate, which are healthy, which are normal.

Even the naming of sexual problems can be extremely difficult. For example, a woman who has difficulty expressing herself sexually is sometimes labeled "frigid." This suggests that she is not an emotional person, or that she can't feel warmth for someone else. Many times, though, what is called "frigid" has nothing to do with emotions and everything to do with physical symptoms. A woman's sexual response and her emotions may be linked somehow. But "frigid" carries strong negative overtones about her completeness as a woman.

Likewise, the word *impotent* may be applied to a man whose desire to have sex ends in frustration. But again, the reasons for his frustration may vary. The problem might have a physical origin, or a psychological one, or both. But the term "impotent"—which means "lacking in power"—suggests his manhood isn't what it should be.

In this volume of the Encyclopedia of Psychological Disorders, the phrase "sexual dysfunction" is used to describe any behavior or response that causes a person to have an unsatisfactory sex life. In clear language, this book provides an overview of sexuality in general and answers the question: What is a sexual disorder? It looks at the physical and psychological reasons for sexual dysfunction, explains fetishes that are dependent on fantasies, and explores disorders in which individuals feel a lack of sexual desire or even an aversion

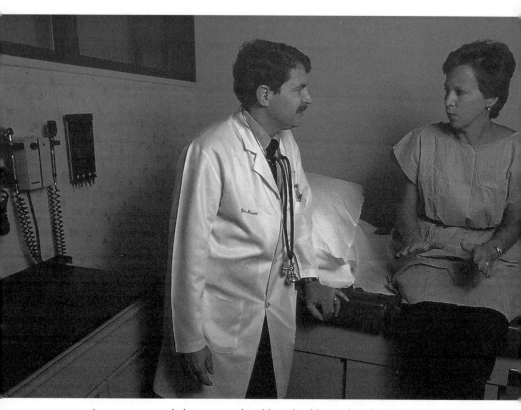

Anyone concerned about a sexual problem should consult a physician, as this woman is doing, instead of drawing conclusions based on incomplete information.

toward sexuality. Sexual disorders that are harmful in some way to self or others are identified as well. Using the latest research studies, the effect of sexual disorders on both individuals and society is examined, and last of all, different treatments for some sexual disorders are discussed.

Sexuality exists on a continuum of behaviors. Occasional divergent behaviors do not mean that an individual has a sexual disorder. However, recent research indicates that nearly everyone, at one time or another, experiences some form of sexual disorder.

Anyone with concerns about his or her sexual behavior should always consult with a physician and not draw conclusions based on limited information. Sexual problems can be treated. What is more, a sexual disorder does not diminish one's overall worth as a human being. A person with a sexual disorder may function successfully in many other areas of life. After all, sexuality is only one facet of our lives as human beings.

Because sexuality is so intimately tied to our concepts of who we are, however, we cannot separate the physical causes and symptoms of sexual disorders from the psychological ones. Our physical responses affect our emotions—and vice versa. This interplay between body and mind, cause and effect, is acknowledged and discussed in the pages that follow.

Sexual disorders involve a wide array of physical and mental processes, and they can put unbearable strain on a relationship. This woman may be conflicted about her own sexuality. She may have a purely physical problem that can be treated medically. Or she may be feeling unloved as a result of her husband's disorder.

1

WHAT IS A SEXUAL DISORDER?

From the standpoint of the human body, sex is complicated. Sexual activity requires the physical coordination of blood, nerves, muscles, and glands. All must work in harmony, the way a hurdler's body must meet the demands created by suddenly leaping to clear a hurdle. In addition, sex is a physical process that is linked to the human mind. People's emotions—desire, love, passion—and their values about what's right for them and what isn't, all play a role in their sexuality—or in other words, their sexual behavior.

Men and women react to sex differently, both physically and psychologically. This means that what seems arousing to men may not be as arousing to women—and vice versa. Take what men and women consider sexy, for example. Men tend to become aroused by visual stimuli—a naked partner, for instance—and by sexual fantasies, as well as by being touched on sensitive areas of the body. Women become aroused by fantasies, too, but touching is more important to women's sexual response than visual stimuli. (Perhaps this explains why magazines for men feature naked models, but practically no women's magazines portray naked men.) Men react more strongly to visual cues, while women respond sexually to emotional tenderness. Clearly, men and women often have very different emotional responses to sexuality.

Just as clearly, men and women have very different sexual organs as well. This means that the physical response for men is not the same as it is for women. In both men and women, *hormones* are important to normal sexual functioning, but the specific levels of hormones are different for males and females. Men have higher levels of the hormone testosterone, while estrogen and progesterone play a greater role in women's sexuality. For both men and women, sexual functioning is a complicated process that relies on many things, including structural, chemical, and emotional factors.

But this still does not answer the question: What is a sexual disorder?

SEXUAL DIFFERENCES BETWEEN MEN AND WOMEN

As Moir and Jessel argue in their book *Brain Sex: The Real Difference Between Men and Women*, the groundwork for the differences between men's and women's sexuality is actually laid extremely early in our development. Moir and Jessel state,

> While the brain is developing in the womb, the hormones control the way the neural networks are laid out. Later on, at puberty, these hormones will revisit the brain to switch on the network they earlier created. Their action is like the process of photography: it is as if a negative is produced in the womb, which is only developed when these chemical messengers return in adolescence. Differences in human [sexual] behavior depend on the interaction between hormones and the brain.

Moir and Jessel go on to note that "a woman is more excited by those senses to which her brain's priorities predispose her . . . while . . . high testosterone, acting upon a male brain, increases . . . the single-minded approach to a problem."

In other words, sexual behaviors are determined in large part by hormones and brain structures. Women and men handle their sexualities differently partly because of the physical differences in their makeup.

A SEXUAL "SHORT-CIRCUIT"

A sexual disorder interferes with the pattern of sexual response. Most researchers of human sexuality recognize four related but separate phases of sexual response: desire, excitement, orgasm, and recovery. Usually, we think of all four as part of one act, especially since books and movies tend to show people going in a straight line from desire to recovery. But each phase can be inhibited—that is, interfered with—in different ways or for different reasons.

Sometimes a trauma or severe shock can disturb all four phases. For instance, a woman who has been sexually attacked at some time in her life might "shut down" to sex completely because of the trauma. A history of *incest, sexual abuse,* or *rape* may thus place an individual at risk for developing sexual problems.

However, a disturbance for any reason in *one or more* of the sexual phases will lead to a kind of sexual short circuit that makes reaching the other phases unlikely or difficult. For example, a man with a serious conflict about whether his sexual desire is socially acceptable may see his inner conflict express itself as failure to have an *erection*. In other words, a basic conflict about desire itself can interfere with one or all of the other phases. In some cases, sexual disorders are just one aspect of a major psychiatric disorder that needs to be addressed, such as depression.

Sexual orientation (that is, whether one is sexually attracted to members of the opposite sex or members of the same sex) is *not* a determining factor in sexual disorders. Heterosexual, homosexual, or bisexual individuals all may experience sexual disorders.

On the physical level, sexual disorders occur for various reasons, including illness. Illnesses that affect sexual functioning include:

- Neurological diseases, such as multiple sclerosis, lumbar or sacral spinal cord trauma, and herniated disks
- Circulatory diseases that can interfere with the arteries or veins of the penis
- Endocrine disorders, such as diabetes
- Liver disease

All of these can result in sexual disorders.

Drugs that affect any part of the body's systems used in sexual activity can also interfere with sexual functioning. Many common medications, such as those used to control high blood pressure, can impair erectile function in men and decrease lubrication in women. Antipsychotics and antidepressants can inhibit these same functions. Some drugs are said to decrease sexual desire itself. These medications include spironolactone (a diuretic taken for high blood pressure) and steroids (anti-inflammatory drugs used for various medical reasons, including immunosuppression and allergies).

WHEN DO SEXUAL DISORDERS OCCUR?

The onset, or occurrence, of sexual disorder may or may not be regular or predictable. Physicians and researchers refer to four types of sexual disorders:

Here, a pharmacist fills a prescription for blood pressure medication. Drugs used to treat a variety of ailments can cause erectile dysfunction or inhibit sexual desire.

- *Lifelong:* The disorder has always been present in the person's life. For example, an individual has been fearful of sexual activity since *puberty.*

- *Acquired:* At some point the person began having the disorder. This individual experienced no sexual disorder until an incident or change caused it.

- *Situational:* The disorder occurs in some situations and not others. An individual feels aroused when alone, for example, but not in the presence of a partner.

- *Generalized*: The disorder occurs regardless of the situation. For example, an individual feels a lack of interest in sex for no particular reason.

Just how many Americans experience sexual disorders is hard to determine, but the evidence indicates that they are common. Citing a survey of 100 well-educated, happily married couples, Hales and his colleagues found that 40 percent of the males reported that at some point during their lives they had problems either achieving an erection or ejaculating, while women reported an even higher incidence of sexual problems. In fact, 63 percent of the women had difficulty at some point in their lives achieving arousal or orgasm. In addition, 50 percent of the men and 77 percent of the women reported other sexual difficulties, including a lack of interest or an inability to relax. The latest sexual research from the National Opinion Research Center indicates that almost a third of all men and a little less than half of all women suffer from some type of sexual dysfunction.

Self-esteem is often closely interwoven with sexual identity. Sexual functioning, however, is a delicate and complicated system that can easily be disturbed by many factors; the presence of a sexual disorder should not take away from an individual's sense of self-worth, nor should it devalue the individual in the eyes of others. As research indicates, a person who experiences a sexual disorder is not abnormal or "weird."

Perhaps if we look at how different cultures think about sexuality, we will have a better foundation for our understanding of the true nature of sexual disorders.

In all cultures around the world, clothing is used to reinforce the sense of being male or female. This Indian mother wears traditional garb appropriate to women, and she has dressed her young son in an unmistakably masculine way.

2

AN OVERVIEW OF SEXUALITY

A wide variety of factors shape a person's sexuality. These factors can be broadly grouped as biological, psychological, and cultural (how a society functions). While human beings all experience the same biological influences over their sexuality, their psychological and cultural influences, which pertain to traditions, laws, and social values, can differ widely.

For instance, cultures vary greatly in terms of societal acceptance of different kinds of sexual behavior. In some societies, children are discouraged from knowing anything about sexuality, and they are not allowed to understand even the basics of sexual reproduction. Other societies encourage children to learn about sex. Parents sometimes exercise their right to educate their children about sex, while at the same time they may discourage open discussions about sex in settings outside the home. Whatever the practice of the individual society, children grow up aware of the parental, religious, and social norms of sexual behavior.

SOCIETAL WAYS OF CONTROLLING SEXUALITY

Throughout history, societies have controlled sexuality in several ways. First, all societies determined that some form of marriage was necessary. Marriage not only removed both partners from the constant competition that surrounds finding mates, but also allowed individuals to devote more time and energy to other necessary and useful tasks of life. In addition, marriage established genetic links; in other words, it established who a child's father was, thus forming the foundation of different cultures' genealogy and inheritance lines. Today, what has come to be called the "nuclear family"—mother, father, and children—remains the basic unit of society throughout the world.

Second, societies have controlled sexuality by dictating whom individuals can marry or have as sexual partners. All societies practiced some combina-

Despite many differences in sexual attitudes and practices, all cultures regulate sexuality through marriage. Here, Korean-American newlyweds bow to each other in a Buddhist temple.

tion of *endogamy*—keeping the choice of a partner within one's group—and *exogamy*—forcing individuals to marry outside the group. This balance kept groups strong through alliances, loyalty, and political power. In addition, all societies have prohibited incest, not usually for genetic reasons (the effects of which are still unknown in many parts of the world), but because duties, rights, and obligations within groups would become too complicated if incest were allowed. This restriction remains in force throughout the world today.

Third, most societies have exercised control over sexuality by allowing exceptions to otherwise widely held sexual rules. Societies usually admit that not all people can conform to the same codes of behavior. Indeed, in the open societies of Europe and North America, where citizens resist interference in their personal lives, it is often difficult to establish just what the codes are. Divorce, for example, is an exception to the bonds of marriage that is permitted in many societies.

Fourth, societies have controlled sexuality by setting the terms of what is appropriate physical behavior. Kissing, for instance, is not practiced in all societies. Some groups believe the proper uses of the mouth are limited to biting, chewing, and speaking; they would never consider using the mouth to demonstrate physical affection. Also, while some societies emphasize the sexual appeal of the female breast, others—such as the Chinese—pay little attention to it. Still other cultures believe putting one's mouth to a woman's breast is only for babies. Although touching the *genitalia* with the hands is a nearly universal behavior, a few groups will not do so because they are repelled by genital secretions. Today, however, information flows across borders through electronic media, and a more traditional society may have difficulty in preventing its members from experimenting with new behavior.

And last, most societies have defined what is appropriate sexually for men versus women. Throughout history, very few societies allowed wives sexual freedom, for example, while it was expected or tolerated in husbands. If the husband gave his permission, however, sex outside of marriage for a woman was another matter. In medieval Europe, it was widely understood that a lord had the right to be the first to sleep with a serf's bride, if the lord wished. Even today, somewhere between two-fifths and three-fifths of preliterate societies (ones that have no written language) permit wife-lending. (In other words, the husband allows the wife to have intercourse with certain relatives, generally his brothers.) In these instances, the main consideration is whether the wife's sexual relationship will bring the husband status and influence. Although our own culture may not practice these particular sexual customs, a double standard of sexual behavior for men and women is still widespread.

THE INFLUENCES OF SOCIAL CLASS AND LAW ON SEXUAL BEHAVIOR

Civilizations are made up of classes—from the poorest and least powerful, to the richest and most powerful. Subgroups in the system normally develop their own values about sexuality. For example, most of the recorded knowledge about sexual behavior and attitudes in ancient cultures comes from the upper or ruling class. The sexual behavior and feelings of the slaves and peasants were seldom noted. Considerable social class differences in sexuality continue to exist today in the United States.

Another influence is law, specifically laws that directly control sexual behavior. Generally, a society's legal system is concerned with the protection of persons or property, and at first glance, laws that control sex may seem to be the exception to this general rule. However, in fact, laws about sex often contain elements of personal or property protection. Historically, women have been considered property, and in other cases, laws have been designed to protect women from male exploitation. In many cases, though, these laws are also about maintaining a society's moral codes and values.

Sex laws may be grouped in three categories:

1. Those concerned with protecting persons; these mainly involve the issue of consent. Rape is an example of an illegal act, because consent is not given.

2. Those designed to prevent offense to the public. These kinds of laws prohibit such activities as sex in public, *exhibitionism*, and open *prostitution*.

Poverty and undying demand make prostitution a serious social problem all over the world. When they are unable to eliminate it, governments may try creative ways to regulate it. For example, prostitutes in Mexico City, shown here, must obey a dress code that forbids them from dressing provocatively before midnight.

SEX AND THE CODE OF HAMMURABI

The earliest records of civilization come from Mesopotamia, an area of the Middle East known today as Iraq. The Code of Hammurabi, an ancient king of this land, dates from around the year 1750 B.C. The Code covered all aspects of the lives of Hammurabi's subjects, including the relations between men and women. As the following excerpts show, marriage was closely tied to issues of money and property, and penalties for breaking the laws were harsh:

- If a man's wife be surprised [having intercourse] with another man, both shall be tied and thrown into the water, but the husband may pardon his wife and the king his slaves.

- If a man violate the wife of another man, who has never known a man, and still lives in her father's house, and sleep with her and be surprised [caught], this man shall be put to death, but the wife is blameless.

- If the "finger is pointed" at a man's wife, but she is not caught sleeping with the other man, she shall jump into the river [for the sake of] her husband.

- If a man wishes to separate from his wife who has borne him no children, he shall give her the amount of her purchase money and the dowry which she brought from her father's house, and let her go.

- If a woman quarrel with her husband, and say : "You are not congenial to me," the reasons for her prejudice must be presented. If she is guiltless, and there is no fault on her part, but he leaves and neglects her, then no guilt attaches to this woman, she shall take her dowry and go back to her father's house. If she is not innocent, but leaves her husband, and ruins her house, neglecting her husband, this woman shall be cast into the water.

3. Those aimed at maintaining sexual morality. These make up the majority of sex laws and cover such behaviors as sex outside marriage, incest, prostitution, *voyeurism*, nudity, *transvestitism*, censorship, and even specific sexual techniques.

In recent years, in Europe and the United States the issue of whether laws should control human sexuality has been widely debated. While most people agree that sex laws are necessary to protect both individuals and society as a whole, others argue that what consenting adults do in private should not be subject to legal control.

WESTERN ATTITUDES ABOUT SEXUALITY

In Western civilization, attempts at studying human sexual behavior date back at least to the ancient Greeks. The physician Hippocrates and the philosophers Plato and Aristotle all offered theories regarding sexual responses and dysfunctions, reproduction and contraception, abortion, sex legislation, and sexual ethics. Greek physicians working in Rome, such as Soranus and Galen, further added to knowledge about human sexuality. The work of these Greeks prompted later Islamic scholars to also devote attention to sexual questions. These Islamic studies, originally written in Arabic, were translated and introduced into medieval Europe. Together with reedited Greek and Roman manuscripts, they became standard texts at newly established medical schools. These texts inspired a rebirth of research on the human body in the 16th, 17th, and 18th centuries.

On the other hand, Western attitudes about sexuality have been greatly influenced by religious values as well. Mainly, these values have come from the Old and New Testaments of the Bible, in addition to the doctrines of the Christian church. Certain historical periods—for instance, the Middle Ages, the era of Puritanism, the Enlightenment, and the Victorian age—have also promoted specific attitudes about sexuality, many of which endure even today. Our culture's current attitudes about sexuality influence our religion, literature, films, paintings, music, television, theater, and formal education.

AMERICAN ATTITUDES ABOUT SEXUALITY

The turn of the 20th century saw a change in the way the Western world looks at sexuality. At that time, the investigation of human sexuality—"sexology," as it came to be called—became an important area of study.

But not until after the Second World War did sexology experience a surge of interest in the United States through the efforts of Alfred C. Kinsey. His training and experience as a zoologist made him well suited for the task of conducting a large-scale survey of actual sexual behavior

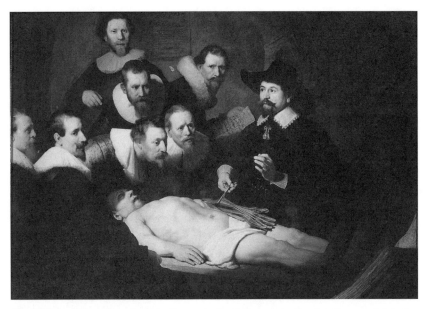

The rebirth of scientific curiosity in Europe in the 16th century stimulated research into the workings of the human body. In this painting by Rembrandt, medical students dissect a cadaver.

among Americans. With two monumental studies, the so-called Kinsey Reports (*Sexual Behavior in the Human Male*, 1948, and *Sexual Behavior in the Human Female*, 1953), Kinsey and his coauthors made new and nonmedical contributions to sex research.

Ernst and Loth, contemporaries of Kinsey, considered that the "Kinsey Report has done for sex what Columbus did for geography." In their 1948 book *American Sexual Behavior and the Kinsey Report*, they went on to say that American

> habits, both of thinking and acting, have been so conditioned by the blind acceptance of standards fitted to another age that we do not know what a practical attitude toward sex should be. What is normal? What is moral? What is pure? How much of our legal code dealing with sex is sensible? What is healthy?
>
> Sex behavior and our attitudes toward it are not set by . . . clergymen, doctors and lawyers. They are set by all the people. The Kinsey Report introduces all the people to some of the facts out of which they themselves will cut the patterns of the future.

In other words, the Kinsey Report told Americans the nature of their actual sexual behaviors and attitudes.

In the 1940s and 1950s, sex-research pioneer Dr. Alfred C. Kinsey published two studies on America's sexual attitudes and behavior. The books created a sensation and reached the bestseller lists.

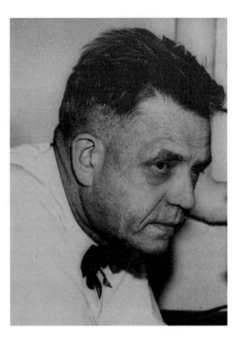

Within two weeks of the 1948 publication of Kinsey's findings on male sexuality, there were 185,000 copies of this scientific study in print, and it had hit the *New York Times'* bestseller list. According to Kinsey and his associates, even they were "totally unprepared" for the results. Kinsey's report included these findings:

- Most men masturbated.
- Most men became sexually active by the age of 15.
- Married men derived less than 90 percent of their sexual outlet from intercourse with their wives.
- At least 95 percent of all males engaged in sexual practices forbidden by many state laws.

Five years later, Kinsey's study on female sexuality revealed that American women were also extremely active sexually, both inside and outside of marriage.

However, Kinsey's findings on homosexuality were what most amazed the American public. According to his report, half the men he interviewed had experienced erotic attraction toward other men, 37 percent had acted on that attraction as adults, over 12 percent had extended same-sex relationships, and 4 percent were exclusively homosexual. Kinsey's study of female sexuality indicated that a high percentage of women were also involved with same-sex relationships.

The public's response to this study was dramatic. Not only did the Kinsey Reports generate a great deal of discussion and controversy about sexuality, but Kinsey himself and his institute came under attack. Funding for the institute's research dried up.

Moreover, Kinsey's methods have been criticized by statistical experts, and the value of his data called into question. It has been said, for example, that whites were overrepresented in his survey, and African Americans and Latinos underrepresented; that 25 percent of his male subjects were prisoners, who made up only 1 percent of the population at the time; and that he paid too much attention to people with unconventional sex lives, since most other people in the late 1940s and early 1950s were unwilling to discuss their personal lives with him, and those who did probably exaggerated.

In the last few decades, scientific attention has again shifted to medical and physiological studies of sex. Mainly as the result of two other pioneering books, *Human Sexual Response* (1966) and *Human Sexual Inadequacy* (1970) by William H. Masters and Virginia Johnson, researchers have concentrated on treating the sexual dysfunctions of both individuals and couples.

In 1994, Edward O. Laumann, John Gagnon, Robert Michael, and S.

Dr. Virginia Johnson, shown in her office in 1997, was a forerunner in the field of sex therapy. With her husband, Dr. William Masters, she published important studies on sexual behavior and established a sex therapy center in St. Louis, Missouri.

Michaels published another survey of sex in America entitled *The Social Organization of Sexuality*. (Robert Michael also published a separate report entitled *Sex in America: A Definitive Survey*.) Unlike some earlier studies, this $1.7 million project relied on a random selection and used lengthy, in-person interviews. The authors stressed that their results indicate the strong relationship between sexuality and other aspects of life. People who reported general unhappiness or stress in their lives were far more likely to have sexual problems—and vice versa.

In general, despite the openness with which Americans discuss their sexuality, most people in our culture have conservative values about sexual behavior. This can be seen perhaps most clearly in the controversies surrounding sex education in schools.

A major role of sex education is to teach the positive nature of sexuality. However, in some communities organized groups of adults oppose sex education in the public schools. They argue that family values about sex are personal and private, and they fear that teachers will influence their students in ways that conflict with family values and beliefs. Classes often include discussions of rape, sexual abuse, abortion, contraception, *masturbation*, sexually transmitted diseases, pregnancy, childbirth, dating, marriage, and family life. Many of these topics draw the fire of conservative groups.

HIGHLIGHTS OF SEX IN AMERICA, A 1994 STUDY BY ROBERT MICHAEL

- For women, some of the most common complaints in regards to sex were loss of desire, difficulties achieving orgasm, and not finding sex pleasurable.
- For men, the number one problem was reaching orgasm too quickly. Problems with erection, lack of desire, and anxiety were also commonly cited by more than 10 percent of the men.
- Single people reported far more sexual problems than married people. Unmarried women were one and a half times more likely to have anxiety or orgasm problems than married women, while unmarried men had significantly higher rates of dysfunction in *all* categories.

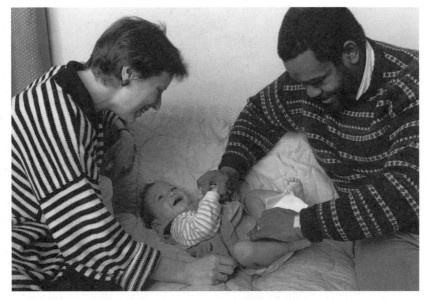

Beginning in the 1950s, public discussion of sexual issues was prompted by profound social changes, including the mixing of groups that historically had been separated. Interracial marriages were illegal in many parts of the United States until the 1960s. Here, a mixed-race couple cares for their infant son.

Nevertheless, despite the resistance from some sectors, several recent historical forces in the United States have caused sexuality to be discussed more widely than ever before. These changes include:

- The rise of feminism, with new attitudes about female sexuality
- An increased acceptance of premarital sex
- An increased acceptance of divorce
- A mixing of social groups that would not have encountered each other even half a century ago, when class, race, and religion often held people in certain social positions for their entire lives. Such increased mixing has introduced Americans to a broader array of opinions, values, and practices in regard to sex.

As a result of these changes in our society, in general Americans today are more tolerant of sexual behavior than they were a generation ago.

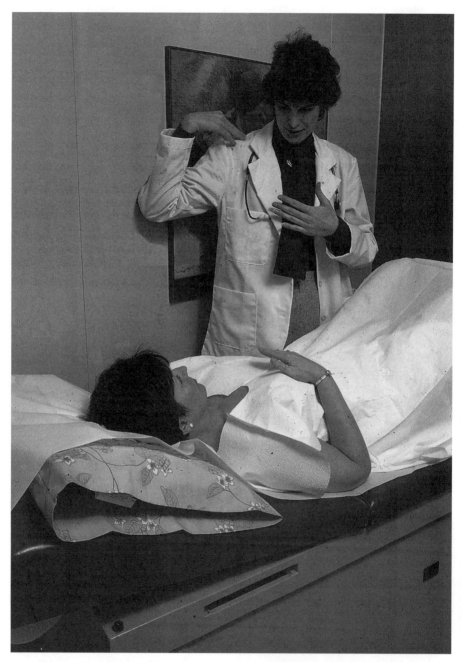

In seeking treatment for sexual disorders, especially those involving physical pain, a woman should first consult her obstetrician or gynecologist, as this woman is doing.

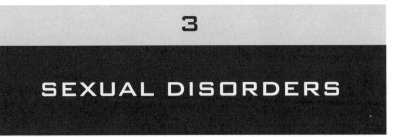

3

SEXUAL DISORDERS

Many sexual disorders have physical symptoms that a specialist can identify. The causes of these problems are complex, however, and very often they are more psychological than physical. Even if the root cause of a disorder is purely physical, its results are so mixed up with emotional responses that separating the psychological from the physical is difficult. If a person's physical response is unsatisfactory—for example, if a man finds he has trouble getting an erection during sex—this can cause distress and problems between partners, which in turn leads to increased psychological distress. Separating the physical from the psychological causes of a particular disorder thus becomes impossible. As a result, most psychologists today use a holistic model—that is, one that looks at human beings in their entirety, rather than dividing them into two pieces, the psychological and the physical.

Keeping that in mind, here are descriptions of sexual disorders by gender.

FEMALE SEXUAL DISORDERS

Female sexual arousal disorder, or *FSAD*, interferes with the arousal part of a woman's sexual response. The American Psychiatric Association, in the most recent edition of its *Diagnostic and Statistical Manual of Mental Disorders* (*DSM-IV*)—a comprehensive guide to mental health problems for health professionals—describes FSAD as the persistent or recurrent inability to attain, or maintain until completion of sexual activity, an adequate lubrication-swelling response. Emotionally, a woman with FSAD usually does not experience sensations that people describe as being "turned on" or "sexy." She may avoid sexual contact altogether; she may feel neutral about it; or she may enjoy it only to a point.

Like most sexual dysfunctions, FSAD may be either lifelong, meaning that the woman has never responded to sexual contact, or acquired, meaning that she formerly responded to sexual contact but doesn't any longer. Her dysfunction might also be situational—occurring sometimes—or it might be generalized, occurring regardless of the situation.

The traits of FSAD can appear in combination, too. For example, a woman who has lifelong and situational FSAD will always have trouble becoming aroused with her partner, but she may be able to become aroused when she is alone. A woman who has acquired and situational FSAD once was able to become aroused, but now she can't. Again, the problem may only exist when she is with her sexual partner; the woman may be able to arouse herself when she is alone. A woman who has life-long and generalized FSAD will always have trouble getting aroused in all situations. And finally, a woman with acquired and generalized FSAD is unable to become aroused regardless of the situation, even though she has not had sexual response problems in the past.

Some of the most common causes of this dysfunction are guilt and hostility. Guilt usually involves an internal conflict between a desire to enjoy sex and an unconscious fear of enjoying it. Hostility often stems from anger at her partner. Obviously, these are not physical causes, and yet they produce a physical result.

The following scenario is a fairly common example of how FSAD can interfere with a married couple's sex life: A wife seeks counseling because she cannot enjoy sex with her husband. She did enjoy sex when they were first married, but gradually she began to feel more and more uncomfortable. During her counseling sessions, she explains that her mother told her that sex was "giving in to" a man, which, according to her mother, was wrong. This message was in direct conflict with her desire to enjoy sex with her husband. As a result, she kept trying to ignore her sexual feelings for her husband as a way of keeping the peace between her thoughts and her body.

A woman with *female orgasmic disorder* may be very sexually aroused but never reach orgasm. Again, female orgasmic disorder can be either lifelong or acquired, situational or generalized. A woman with this disorder never has an orgasm.

The *DSM IV* describes female orgasmic disorder as the persistent or recurrent delay in, or absence of, orgasm in a female following a normal sexual excitement phase. However, researchers point out that women have differences in the type or intensity of stimulation that triggers orgasm. The diagnosis of female orgasmic disorder should be based on a physician's judgment about what would be a reasonable response,

Attitudes that can interfere with a couple's sex life, such as guilt or hostility, often come to light during counseling sessions. These married people are discussing the intimate details of their life with their therapist.

given the woman's age and sexual experience. In other words, not all women must respond in the same standard way to sex activity; some women may be perfectly satisfied and sexually fulfilled with sexual experiences that others would consider less than adequate. Once again, the diagnosis of this disorder cannot be based on clearly defined physical criteria.

Female orgasmic disorder may have any one of several causes. For instance, the woman might pressure herself with her belief that having an orgasm is very important, which can interfere with her response. Or she might be uncomfortable, angry, or distressed, which will affect her ability to reach orgasm. On the other hand, she might not have a partner who meets or understands her sexual needs.

Dyspareunia is genital pain associated with intercourse. It may occur before, during, or after intercourse. The pain may be slight or sharp; however, it must be significant enough to cause distress in a woman for it to be considered a disorder. In addition, to be considered dyspareunia, the disturbance cannot be caused by drugs, lack of lubrication, a medical condition, or another sexual disorder. Like other disorders, it can be lifelong, situational, acquired, or generalized.

A medical condition, such as a urinary tract infection or scar tissue, can also cause the disorder. Also, some medications have been known to produce painful orgasms. The reasons for dyspareunia may be psychological, and repeat episodes of pain associated with intercourse can lead to anxiety. Most women seek treatment for dyspareunia from an obstetrician or *gynecologist.*

Vaginismus is an involuntary spasm at the entrance of the *vagina* that makes intercourse impossible. This is generally thought to be a fairly rare disorder. The *DSM-IV* defines vaginismus as a recurrent or persistent involuntary spasm of the musculature of the outer third of the vagina, interfering with sexual intercourse.

Vaginismus is often the result of a trauma associated in a woman's mind with the act of intercourse. A sexual assault, painful experiences with intercourse, or a traumatic pelvic exam might be the psychological reason for vaginismus. Other causes can be pelvic disease and anxiety.

MALE SEXUAL DISORDERS

Erectile dysfunction is the impairment of the erectile reflex. In other words, a man with this disorder is unable to have or maintain an erection, a symptom that can be physically observed. According to the American Psychiatric Press *Textbook of Psychiatry* (1999) by Hales, Yudofsky, and Talbott, another criterion for this disorder is the "marked distress or interpersonal difficulty" that it causes. Like other dysfunctions, erectile dysfunction can be either lifelong or acquired, situational or generalized.

A man who has never had an erection has lifelong erectile dysfunction. A man who has had erections in the past but is no longer able to have or maintain them has acquired erectile dysfunction. As a situational dysfunction, erectile dysfunction is very common. At some time in his life, any man will be unable to have an erection even though he wants to. This is not a sign of a disorder. The *DSM-IV* limits erectile disorder to a persistent or recurrent inability to attain or maintain an erection until completion of the sexual activity.

Erectile dysfunction is more likely than the other dysfunctions to

Drugs are a major cause of erectile dysfunction. By abusing alcohol, this young man is putting his long-term sexual health at risk.

have a physical cause. Drugs (especially alcohol), diabetes, Parkinson's disease, multiple sclerosis, and spinal cord lesions can all be causes of erectile dysfunction. Sometimes a prescribed medicine, such as blood pressure medicine, might have a side effect that causes this disorder.

From a psychological standpoint, however, the most likely cause of erectile dysfunction is anxiety. Sexual activity makes most people nervous, excited, or anxious. Sometimes these feelings can cause a man to lose his erection, or to fail to achieve it.

Male orgasmic disorder is an involuntary interference with the male's ability to *ejaculate*. A man cannot have an orgasm, in other words. As with the other dysfunctions, the man can experience this disorder as lifelong, acquired, situational, or generalized. The *DSM-IV* describes male orgasmic disorder as a persistent or recurrent delay in, or absence of, orgasm following a normal sexual excitement phase during sexual activity. However, the *DSM-IV* adds that a physician must take into account the person's age and sexual behavior.

The man who has never ejaculated at all, even during masturbation,

The most common psychological cause of erectile dysfunction is anxiety. The stress on this overworked individual may interfere with his ability to achieve or maintain an erection.

is rare, for often men, like women, who are unable to achieve orgasm with a partner can do so when alone. The cause of this dysfunction is rarely physical, although the problem shows up as a physical and observable symptom.

According to experts, more often than not the cause of male orgasmic disorder is a traumatic sexual experience, strict religious upbringing, hostility, too much self-control, or lack of trust in a partner. Many problems connected with this disorder are treatable with sex therapy.

Premature ejaculation is defined by the American Psychiatric Association as "persistent or recurrent ejaculation with minimal sexual stimulation before, during, or shortly after penetration and before the person wishes it." Exactly what causes premature ejaculation is not clear.

A number of possible explanations exist. Physical causes are not common, but sometimes nerve sensitivity in a man's penis can lead to premature ejaculation. Also, some infections of the urinary tract are possible causes of premature ejaculation, as are certain drugs. More often, though, the man has not learned to pay attention to his own body signals. Some men will not give themselves permission to feel erotic, or they will ignore their feelings until overcome with an orgasm. Other men have conditioned themselves to get sex over with quickly. Treatment through sex therapy is often recommended for premature ejaculation.

Premature ejaculation is also a relative term, since much depends on the satisfaction of the man's partner. After all, if a man ejaculates quickly, why exactly is this considered "premature"? If his partner is able to achieve orgasm just as quickly, then both partners may be perfectly satisfied with his sexual performance.

In the next chapter, we will look at sexual disorders that lie less in the objective, physical realm and more in the realm of fantasy.

In 1995, a group of young women in Quezon City demonstrated before the Philippine Congress, demanding greater efforts to control child prostitution and harsher penalties for pedophiles. The women wore hoods because they themselves were child prostitutes who had been the victims of pedophiles, and they feared having their identities known.

4

SEXUAL DISORDERS BASED ON FANTASIES

Many sexual problems fall into the category of paraphiliac disorders, which are characterized by strong sexual urges and sexually arousing fantasies. According to the *DSM-IV*, these urges and fantasies generally involve:

1. Nonhuman objects
2. The suffering or humiliation of oneself or one's partner
3. Children or other nonconsenting persons.

The urges or fantasies must occur over a period of at least six months. Some individuals must have these fantasies to be sexually aroused; in other words, all their sexual activities involve these fantasies in some way. In other cases, however, individuals may merely have episodes of paraphiliac fantasies (for instance, during periods of stress); the rest of the time, these people may be able to function sexually without the paraphiliac stimuli.

The following are examples of paraphilias:

- Fetishism (sexual arousal to nonliving objects such as female undergarments)
- Transvestic fetishism (sexual urges and fantasies involving cross-dressing)
- Pedophilia (sexual urges and fantasies involving prepubescent children)
- Sexual sadism (sexual urges and acted-out fantasies—real, not imagined—in which hurting or humiliating someone is sexually exciting to the person in control)
- Sexual masochism (sexual excitement caused by being humiliated, beaten, bound, or hurt)

The following paraphilias involve unknowing partners:

- Exhibitionism (showing one's genitals to an unsuspecting stranger)
- Voyeurism (watching an unsuspecting person who is naked or undressing)
- Frottage (becoming sexually aroused by rubbing up against a stranger)

All of these disorders will be discussed in depth below.

Many persons with paraphilias say these acts do not cause them personal distress. Others report extreme guilt, shame, and depression at having to engage in an unusual sexual activity that is socially unacceptable or that they consider to be immoral. Persons who have these disorders usually come for treatment because their partners or families insist, or because authorities order them to seek treatment.

The reason that individuals with these disorders are brought to public attention is because of the potential for harm they involve. Sexual offenses against children comprise a large percentage of all reported criminal sex acts, and individuals with exhibitionism, pedophilia, and voyeurism make up the majority of apprehended sex offenders. In some situations, acting out paraphiliac urges may lead to self-injury, such as in sexual masochism. In addition, social and sexual relationships may suffer if others find the unusual sexual behavior shameful or distressing. Frequent, unprotected sex with strangers may result in infection or transmission of a sexually transmitted disease.

Some individuals with a paraphilia select an occupation, hobby, or kind of volunteer work that brings them into contact with the stimulus they desire—selling women's lingerie, for example (fetishism), or working with children (pedophilia). They may purchase or collect photographs, films, and books that focus on the type of paraphilia that appeals to them.

Most persons with these disorders are male. According to the 1999 study by Hales, Yudofsky, and Talbott, for example, among reported cases of sexual abuse of children, over 90 percent of offenders are male. Except for sexual masochism, where the gender ratio is estimated to be 20 males for each female, the other paraphilias are almost never diagnosed in females. The *DSM-IV* indicates that over half of all people with paraphilias begin acting on their sexual urges before age 13.

At one time, people with paraphilias were thought to act out only one type of abnormal sexual behavior. Recent studies, however, suggest that many times these individuals practice more than one paraphilia. Paraphiliac disorders tend to be chronic, ongoing, and lifelong. But both the fantasies and the behaviors often diminish with advancing age.

WHAT CAUSES PARAPHILIAC DISORDERS?

Several theories have been offered to explain the causes of paraphilias. For example, animals that have had part of their *limbic systems* removed show abnormal sexual behavior. (The limbic system includes the structures in the brain that regulate the emotions.) A study by Kolarksy and colleagues cited in Langevin's book *Erotic Preference, Gender Identity, and Aggression in Men* indicates that a higher than normal percentage of paraphilias were seen in a group with *epilepsy* of the temporal lobe. (Epilepsy is a nervous disorder in which the electrical impulses in the brain are disturbed, resulting in uncontrollable seizures. It may originate in different parts of the brain, including the temporal lobes, the sections of the brain located on the sides of the head.)

In *The Psychology of Sexual Diversity*, Howells stated that he found "growing evidence that some fetishisms, as well as other kinds of com-

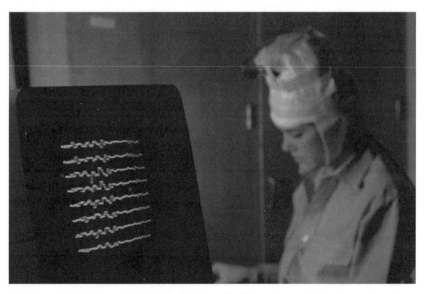

Here, a patient receives a brain scan for signs of epilepsy. Research has shown that a higher than normal percentage of paraphilia occurs in men with epilepsy of the temporal lobe.

pulsive sexual behaviors, may be traced to subtle brain damage of the kind that also gives rise to epilepsy. The damage that is apparently most likely to disrupt sexual behavior is that located in the temporal lobe." This sort of brain damage could be caused by injury during birth (for example, during a forceps delivery) or from illness during the first year or two of life (for example, infantile meningitis). Research like this suggests that paraphilias might have biological origins.

Brain diseases have caused similar abnormal behaviors in humans. Researchers also suggest that high levels of androgens may contribute to inappropriate sexual arousal. Genetic factors may play a role in sexual behavior as well. Howells reports that some studies indicate "remarkable similar fetishistic or transvestic behavior" in identical twins.

On the other hand, just because brain damage and other physiological causes *can* contribute to sexual differences, that does not mean they are the *only* factors involved. As we said, human sexuality is a complicated facet of personality, and our bodies and that which we call our "hearts" cannot be split into separate, neat packages. Many factors may contribute to a sexual problem.

Howells suggests that learning and *conditioning* play a part in an individual's sexual responses. He cites studies that demonstrate that sexual arousal could be conditioned in the laboratory when a group of normal men were taught to associate a picture of a boat with pictures of nude women. In real life, this might mean that an individual's early experiences conditioned that person to connect a certain apparently nonsexual object or activity with sexual arousal.

Imprinting, a process that fixes some concept permanently in a person's memory, is another way of thinking about this, but imprinting goes beyond simple conditioning and involves the basic neural wiring of a person's brain. Howells found that males who had had traumatic childhood experiences were more inclined to associate sexual arousal with something other than simply being close to a woman's body, as though their natural responses had been somehow distorted. Interestingly, research indicated that the traumatic event could take the form of a minor injury to the brain, or accidental but significant experiences with people and articles in the individual's environment—or some combination of the two, demonstrating once again the interplay between physiology and psychology. Howells points again to a connection between the brain's limbic circuits and sexuality; damage to either the right or left side of a man's brain can give rise to decreased sexuality and impotence, but damage specifically to the left side of the brain is more apt to result in bizarre or unusual targets for arousal.

Howells also indicates that female rejection may play a role in some men's sexual problems. In one study, 30 male students were told they had been turned down by "girlfriends" they had selected from photographs, while another group of 30 students were told the girls they had chosen returned their interest. The two groups of men were then asked to rate the attractiveness of various photos that ranged from abstract designs to pictures of underwear, feet, legs, and a complete female body. The "rejected" men showed an increased interest in underwear, feet, and legs, while they had less interest in the whole woman.

Finally, many individuals with paraphilia report having inadequate social skills as a result of the family environment in which they were raised. Some have trouble relating to other adults or to persons of the opposite sex. Others have belief systems that put them outside normal society and thus refuse to consider their behavior inappropriate, arguing for instance that voyeurism "doesn't bother anyone." A study cited in *Erotic Preference, Gender Identity, and Aggression in Men* indicates that voyeurs in particular are apt to come from families with disturbed parent-child relationships. As children, these men tended to be emotionally distant from both parents; their mothers and fathers were apt to have been aggressive both to each other and to their children and also tended to have a higher incidence of mental illness.

These studies all point to some of the specific factors associated with paraphilia, but in reality often a particular paraphilia may be caused by a combination of several of these factors.

TYPES OF PARAPHILIA

Here are descriptions of commonly diagnosed paraphilias:

Exhibitionism involves the exposure of one's genitals to a stranger. Sometimes the individual masturbates while exposing himself (or while fantasizing about exposing himself). If the person acts on these urges, he generally does not attempt further sexual activity with the stranger. In some cases, the individual wants to surprise or shock the observer. In other cases, he fantasizes that the observer will become sexually aroused. Episodes of exhibitionism usually occur before the age of 18, although

Frotteurism is the act of deriving pleasure from touching or rubbing an unwilling person. To avoid capture, a person with this disorder will usually perform the act in a crowded, public place, such as this subway car.

they can begin later, too. Few arrests are made in older age groups, which may suggest that the disorder becomes less severe by middle age.

Fetishism involves the use of nonliving objects (the fetish) for sexual arousal. Among the more common fetish objects are women's underpants, bras, stockings, shoes, boots, or other apparel. The person with a fetish frequently masturbates while holding, rubbing, or smelling the fetish object, or he may ask the sexual partner to wear the object during their sexual encounters. Usually the fetish is needed or strongly preferred for sexual excitement. Without it, males may be unable to get an erection. Physicians do not diagnose fetishism when the object has been designed to be sexually stimulating, however. Usually fetishism begins in adolescence, although the fetish may have been given special significance earlier in childhood because of a certain incident or because of reinforcement by others. Once established, fetishism tends to be chronic or ongoing.

Frotteurism involves touching and rubbing against a nonconsenting person. The behavior usually occurs in crowded places from which the individual can escape arrest—for example, on public transportation or in busy malls. He rubs his genitals against the victim's thighs and buttocks or fondles her with his hands, and while doing this he usually fantasizes that the victim enjoys this and cares about him. However, he also recognizes that this behavior could lead to his arrest, and so he knows he must escape undetected. Usually frotteurism begins in adolescence. Most acts of frottage occur when the person is between 15 and 25 years old, after which there is a gradual decline in number of occurrences.

Pedophilia—the sexual molestation of children—is the most common paraphiliac act involving touching someone against his or her will, or victimizing someone who is unable to give consent. (The legal and medical communities maintain that children cannot knowingly give consent to sex.)

According to the *DSM-IV*, an individual diagnosed with pedophilia must be 16 years old or older, and at least five years older than the child involved. As Abel and Osborn reported in 1995, among children under age 14 who have been molested, females were usually the focus when the victim was not touched (voyeurism, exhibitionism). When the victim

These boys are at the age at which they are most likely to become the victims of pedophiles. Research shows that most pedophiles prey on girls aged 8 to 10, or on boys who are slightly older.

was touched, however, 62 percent of the children were male (Abel and Osborn, 1995).

Conservative estimates indicate that 20 percent of all females and 10 percent of all males have been molested before age 18. In a nationwide study of females in the United States, researchers estimated that 21 million adult females have been sexually assaulted—60 percent before age 18. According to Abel and Osborn, however, pedophilia involving female victims is reported more often than pedophilia involving male victims.

Persons with pedophilia generally report an attraction to children of a particular age. Some individuals prefer males, others females, and some are aroused by both males and females. Those attracted to females usually prefer 8- to 10-year-olds, whereas those attracted to males usually prefer slightly older children. According to the *DSM-IV*, some pedophiles are sexually attracted only to children; others are sometimes attracted to adults as well.

Individuals with pedophilia who act on their urges with children may limit their activity to undressing the child and looking, exposing themselves, masturbating in the presence of the child, or gently touching and fondling the child. Others violate the child sexually. Pedophiles tend to make excuses for their behavior by explaining that their actions had "educational value" for the child, or that the child derived "sexual pleasure" from them, or that the child meant to be "sexually provocative."

Pedophiles report that most of their molestations do not involve incest, but instead are done to children outside their family. Some threaten the child to prevent being discovered. Others, especially those who frequently victimize children, develop methods for obtaining access to children, which can include winning the trust of a child's mother or even marrying her. Often, the molester will be attentive to the child in order to win the child's affection and loyalty, so that the sexual activity can be a secret between them.

Pedophilia usually begins in adolescence, although some individuals report they did not become aroused by children until middle age. Pedophiles tend to act on their urges when they are experiencing psychological or social stress. As a disorder, pedophilia is usually chronic, especially in pedophiles attracted to males.

Sexual masochism involves sexual arousal from the act (real, not imagined) of being humiliated, beaten, bound, or otherwise made to suffer. Some people with this paraphilia feel upset by their fantasies, which usually involve being powerless against a sexual attack. Others act privately on their masochistic sexual urges by deliberately causing themselves physical pain. Masochistic acts involving a partner's help include restraint (physical bondage), blindfolding (sensory bondage), hitting, whipping, beating, electrical shocks, cutting, and humiliation through forced cross-dressing. A masochistic person may want to be treated as a helpless infant and clothed in diapers (infantilism). An especially dangerous form of sexual masochism involves being suffocated, which has resulted in a number of accidental deaths.

Masochistic sexual fantasies are likely to have been present in someone since childhood. Although masochistic activities with partners can begin at various ages, they often begin by early adulthood. Sexual masochism is usually chronic or ongoing, and the person tends to repeat the same masochistic act over and over. Some individuals may engage in masochistic acts for many years without increasing the likelihood of serious injury, while others perform more and more harmful masochistic acts over time, which can cause injury or even death. Some males with sexual masochism also have fetishism, transvestic fetishism, or sexual sadism.

Sexual sadism involves acts (real, not imagined) in which the person becomes sexually excited by inflicting psychological or physical suffering on someone else. Some individuals with this paraphilia feel upset by their sadistic fantasies, which usually are about having power over a victim who is terrified at being helpless. Individuals with this paraphilia sometimes find partners with sexual masochism who are willing to be victims; others act on their sadistic sexual urges with nonconsenting victims. In all cases, it is the suffering of the victim that is sexually exciting. Sadistic fantasies, like masochistic fantasies, are usually about harm or humiliation, such as hitting, cutting, blindfolding, or torturing.

Individuals with this paraphilia usually begin experiencing sadistic sexual fantasies during childhood. Acts of sexual sadism commonly start during young adulthood. Usually, sexual sadism is a chronic paraphilia. When it is practiced with nonconsenting partners, the behavior tends to continue until the person is arrested. Some individuals may engage in sadistic acts for many years without feeling the need to make the activities more harmful; however, often the harshness of the acts increases over time. Persons with severe sexual sadism may seriously injure or kill their victims.

Transvestic fetishism involves cross-dressing—wearing the clothes of the opposite sex. This disorder has been identified only in heterosexual males.

Transvestic behavior can range from occasionally wearing women's clothes to centering one's life around cross-dressing. Men with transvestic fetishism usually have collections of female clothes they use for cross-dressing. Some wear only one item of women's clothing—underwear or blouses, for example—under their otherwise ordinary masculine clothes. Others dress as women, wear makeup, and participate in society looking like females. When not cross-dressed, males with this paraphilia do not look different from other men. Most are heterosexual and have sexual partners, and not often homosexual ones. Some individuals with this disorder also have sexual masochism.

Transvestic fetishism typically begins in childhood or early adolescence. Many cross-dressers do not appear in public until adulthood; when they do, they may wear only a favorite item of women's clothing, or they may cross-dress completely. Often, limited cross-dressing progresses to complete cross-dressing. Many transvestites will try to "purge" themselves of the desire to cross-dress by destroying their collections of female clothes.

Some transvestites report that the urge to cross-dress is affected by circumstances in their lives. Cross-dressers have said that during periods of anxiety or depression, wearing women's clothes will bring them positive feelings—comfort, relief from tension, escape from the pressures of being masculine, feelings of being attractive and beautiful, or sexual excitement. Over 90 percent of 851 cross-dressers in Brown's 1995 study reported feeling euphoric (in other words, extremely happy) when assuming the role of the opposite gender. Many older transvestites reported the need to express an inner, feminine self by cross-dressing.

A person who cross-dresses is not usually confused about his gender identity. In other words, he thinks of himself as a male who happens to respond sexually to putting on female clothing. Sometimes, however, cross-dressing is a sign of a deeper gender identity disorder. A small number of transvestites are actually transsexuals—men who wish to live permanently as females; these individuals may even undergo surgical procedures to change their gender. When cross-dressers do experience a gender identity disorder, they often go into therapy, or are brought for treatment by friends or family members.

We need to keep in mind, however, that someone who dresses provocatively in clothes of the opposite sex cannot automatically be said to have a disorder. A physician probably would diagnose transvestitism if a heterosexual male, over a period of at least six months, had recurrent intense sexual urges and sexually arousing fantasies involving cross-dressing, which he has acted on, or if such thoughts cause him distress. Interestingly, our culture would not consider a woman who dresses in men's clothing to be sexually inappropriate, and women who do so do not find men's clothing to be arousing. This raises questions about the role of culture and gender in the conditioning of unusual sexual responses.

Voyeurism involves observing unsuspecting individuals, usually strangers, who are naked, in the process of undressing, or engaging in sexual activity. The act of watching, or peeping, is done for the purpose of becoming sexually aroused, and generally no contact is sought with the person being watched. Individuals with this disorder may masturbate while they watch, or they may masturbate later when remembering the situation. Often voyeurs fantasize about having a sexual experience with the person they are watching, but this rarely happens. For some voyeurs, watching others is the only form of sexual activity in their lives.

Voyeuristic behavior usually occurs for the first time before age 15. Voyeurism tends to be a chronic or ongoing disorder.

Governor Christie Todd Whitman of New Jersey (right) meets with Maureen Kanka, whose daughter Megan was murdered by a pedophile who had been released from prison. The crime led Mrs. Kanka to advocate the passage of what came to be known as "Megan's Law," which requires that sex offenders register with police upon moving into a community.

CRIMINAL SEXUAL BEHAVIOR

Not all people with sexual disorders engage in criminal activity, but findings from the Bureau of Justice Statistics do indicate that many individuals need treatment for harmful sexual behaviors. On a given day in 1994, the latest year for which statistics are available, approximately 234,000 offenders were convicted of rape or sexual assault. Some of these were remanded to the care, custody, or control of corrections agencies, but nearly 60 percent of these sex offenders were under conditional supervision in the community.

Victims of imprisoned sexual assaulters had a median age of less than 13 years. On average, offenders who had victimized a child were five years older than those who had committed their sexual crimes against an adult. Nearly 25 percent of child victimizers were age 40 or older, but only about 10 percent of the inmates with adult victims fell in that age range.

The median age of rape victims was about 22 years. An estimated 24 percent of those serving time for rape and 19 percent of those serving time for sexual assault had been on probation or parole at the time of the offense for which they were in state prison in 1991.

CONCLUSION

Although paraphilia is a relatively common disorder, we must remember not to "see paraphilia" everywhere. Sexual idiosyncrasies are not necessarily disorders. All human sexuality includes a range of behaviors, and thus the diagnosis of a disorder is not determined by some absolute criterion. Keep in mind that the key element in the diagnosis of a paraphilia is one of these two factors:

1. Abnormal urges or behaviors in the way a person becomes sexually excited
2. Sexual behavior with persons who have not given their consent.

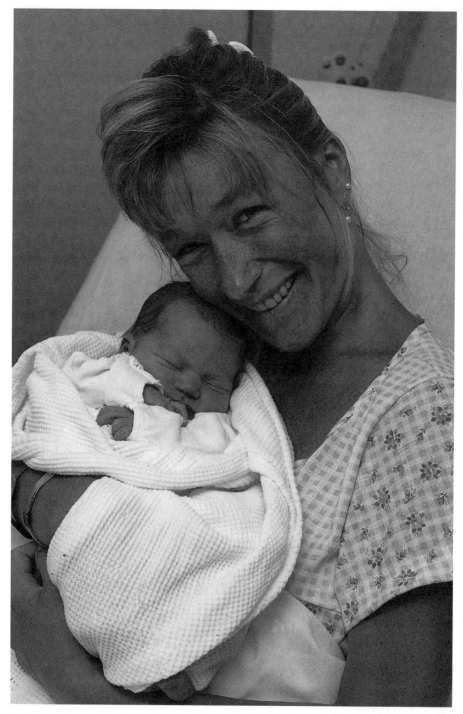

A decrease in sexual desire can be caused by major life changes such as childbirth. This new mother may be prone to the problem known as hypoactive sexual desire disorder.

5

LACK OF DESIRE, AND AVERSION, AS SEXUAL DISORDERS

Mature human beings' interest in sex is normal and a sign of mental health. When individuals' interest in sex is weak, or completely absent, a sexual desire disorder may be the diagnosis.

TWO TYPES OF SEXUAL DESIRE DISORDERS

The widely recognized types of sexual desire disorders are hypoactive sexual desire disorder and sexual aversion disorder.

Hypoactive sexual desire disorder is a set of symptoms that can be summarized as a "quiet" lack of sexual desire. The *DSM-IV* describes this disorder as "persistent or recurrent deficient (or absent) sexual fantasies and desire for sexual activity." Signs include a low rate of sexual activity, and a self-reported lack of desire for sexual activity, an absence of sexual dreams and fantasies, and the failure to notice attractive potential partners.

Keep in mind, however, that people go through phases in their sex lives, depending on internal and external factors. A physician must be the one to make a judgment about the individual's interest in sex based on the patient's age, sex, and life events. For example, a physician would need to rule out the possibility of another physical or psychological complication before diagnosing hypoactive sexual desire disorder.

Hypoactive sexual desire disorder (also known as inhibited sexual desire, or ISD) causes significant distress or interpersonal difficulty. In fact, a physician will diagnose a sexual disorder only if a patient is distressed. Desire differs for each individual, and that difference, even if it means a very cautious sex life, does not necessarily indicate ISD. As one researcher has said, "Only when lack of sexual interest is a source of personal or relationship distress, instead of voluntary choice, is it classified as ISD." Typically, patients with ISD have either no appetite for sex at all (not by choice) or no interest in sex with their

CAUSES OF DECREASED SEXUAL DESIRE

Physical
- Hormone deficiencies
- Clinical depression
- Stress
- Alcoholism
- Kidney failure
- Chronic illness
- Certain drugs or medications

Psychological
- Relationship problems (power struggles, conflict, hostility, etc.)
- Sexual trauma, such as rape
- Major life changes, including the death of a family member, childbirth, or geographic relocation

Often, having negative memories about sexual experiences will also cause hypoactive sexual disorder. People who associate sex with being angry or afraid do not usually encourage sexual intimacy.

partners. They find they can behave as a normally functioning sexual partner, but the experience isn't pleasurable or satisfying. They complain of feeling emotionally separate from the experience.

Hypoactive sexual desire disorder can seriously interfere with a couple's sexual relationship. Here is a fairly typical example that a husband and wife might share with a physician: The wife says that since the birth of her child, she is not interested in sex with her husband. She believes that a mother should not behave in a sexual manner. In addition, her husband has gained quite a bit of weight since the birth of the child, and she finds him less attractive. Her solution to both problems is to "shut down" sexually and avoid sexual contact with her husband. Clearly, her lack of interest will have serious ramifications on her own emotional well-being and on the well-being of the marriage relationship.

Hypoactive sexual desire disorder may be lifelong, appear unexpectedly after a period of normal sexual behavior, or occur only in certain situations—only with the person's partner, for instance. Identifying

Psychological causes of inhibited sexual desire include grief over the death of a loved one, such as this young woman is experiencing.

patients with the disorder requires a medical workup, a psychological evaluation, and an evaluation of the relationship.

Sexual aversion disorder is recognized by intense, constantly occurring or reoccurring feelings of extreme disgust for and avoidance of all—or practically all—genital sexual contact with a partner. This disorder causes serious distress or interpersonal difficulties. Researchers have

Sexual aversion disorder, the intense and recurring disgust toward sexual contact, may be caused by traumatic events connected with sex, such as rape. This woman is trying to escape a danger that could leave her psychologically scarred for life.

found that sexual aversion disorder may have its roots in earlier traumatic and fearful events connected with the sexual act.

In 1995, Kaplan "found a high rate of concordance between anxiety disorders and sexual aversions or phobias in our patient population." Furthermore, she wrote, "more than 25 percent of the 373 patients with sexual anxiety states (sexual aversions or the phobic avoidance of sex) whom we saw between 1976 and 1986, met the *DSM-III* (American Psychiatric Association, 1980) criteria for panic disorder, whereas another 25 percent of these patients showed signs and symptoms of other types of anxiety disorders." Because sex is an interaction between people that requires intimacy and self-assurance, Kaplan makes the logical point that "in extremely anxious individuals, the association between fear and sex is particularly intense, tenacious, and difficult to extinguish."

The 1995 research of Foa, Riggs, and Gershuny also detected a connection between the effect of earlier traumatic sexual or emotional experiences with sexual aversion disorder. They point out that one of the key behaviors of an individual with post-traumatic stress disorder is to shut out unwanted feelings by means of "emotional numbing" to avoid reexperiencing the trauma. These researchers suggest that a person who struggles with memories of a sexual trauma will engage in a cycle of emotional numbing and sexual aversion to cope with feelings of anxiety.

As with other disorders, the first step in identifying the causes of a sexual problem is to seek a physician's help in diagnosing symptoms of either hypoactive sexual disorder or sexual aversion disorder.

This young and apparently happy couple may not believe they are at risk for a sexual problem, but research suggests they may be. "Everyone is at risk of sexual dysfunction, sooner or later," said sex researcher Edward O. Laumann in Newsweek magazine. "It's a myth that young, healthy people aren't going to have sexual problems."

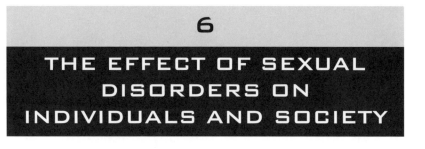

6

THE EFFECT OF SEXUAL DISORDERS ON INDIVIDUALS AND SOCIETY

How widespread are sexual disorders among Americans? A number of major studies of Americans' sexuality have been written in the last 50 years. The most recent, "Sexual Dysfunction in the United States," is the first population-based survey on sexual dysfunction since the famous Kinsey Reports in the late 1940s and early 1950s. This newest research, published in the *Journal of the American Medical Association* in 1999, indicates that sexual disorders are very common among Americans, despite a willingness to be more open about sex than in the past (see Chapter 2).

According to the study, which is based on interviews with more than 3,000 adults, at any given time nearly a third of American men and 4 out of 10 American women suffer some kind of sexual dysfunction, ranging from lack of desire and performance anxiety to problems with arousal and orgasm, and pain during intercourse. As Herbert wrote in *U.S. News & World Report* in 1999, statistically this means that *every* American is likely to confront some form of sexual dysfunction at some time.

Overall, 43 percent of American women and 31 percent of men experience sexual disorders. In an article by John Leland in *Newsweek*, Laumann commented that "the stunning thing is that everyone is at risk of sexual dysfunction, sooner or later. It's a myth that young, healthy people aren't going to have sexual problems."

WHAT THE SURVEY SUGGESTS

Laumann and his colleagues drew their conclusions from data on sexual dysfunction in the National Health and Social Life Survey (NHSLS), conducted in 1992 by the National Opinion and Research Center. Although the survey's interviewers didn't ask people questions about their psychiatric background, they did ask generally about emotional satisfaction and happiness. The data suggest that sexual health is directly tied to the rest of our mental and physical well-being. For example, women who had trouble becoming sexually aroused were five times as likely to be unhappy with their lives as those with no sexual problems. Men who had problems achieving or keeping an erection were more than four times as likely to be unhappy.

According to some experts, these results may also point to the conclusion that depression contributes to sexual disorders—and that depression is a mental health problem that needs to be addressed before a sexual problem can be treated. Commenting on the study in an article by Wray Herbert in *U.S. News & World Report,* Harvard psychiatrist John Ratey concluded that a subclinical (barely noticeable to physicians), or "shadow," depression is most likely at the root of many sexual problems.

In addition, many specialists say that their experiences treating patients indicate that relationship problems play a factor in creating sexual dissatisfaction, too, which may also partly explain the link between unhappiness and sexual disorders. Dr. Richard Kogan, a New York psychiatrist and sex therapist, quoted in Leland's *Newsweek* article, remarked that for women, fixing the sexual problem with a partner means fixing the relationship—or "establishing proper conditions for good sexuality."

THE SURVEY'S FINDINGS

Here is a summary of what the study found:

- In general, married people report better sexual health than singles.

- Overall, the prevalence of sexual dysfunction is higher for women than men (43 percent versus 31 percent).

- In most categories, women have fewer problems as they get older; men often have more.

- Unexpectedly, the more education people have, the fewer sexual problems they report. This is true for both sexes.

- Black women tend to have higher rates of low sexual desire and experience less pleasure compared with white women, who are more likely to have sexual pain than black women. Hispanic women, in contrast, consistently report lower rates of sexual problems than women in other ethnic groups. The

These young people are reducing their risk of sexual disorder simply by getting married. In the National Health and Social Life Survey, conducted in 1992, married people reported better sexual health than singles.

variations among men from different ethnic groups are not as marked but are generally consistent with what women experience.

- Health problems affect women and men differently. Men with poor health have elevated risk for all categories of sexual dysfunction, whereas this factor is only associated with sexual pain for women.

- Women who have been victims of sexual abuse through adult-child contact or through forced sexual contact are more likely to experience arousal disorder. Male victims of adult-child sexual contact are also more likely to have sexual problems than those who have not been victims of such contact.

- Men who have sexually assaulted women are three-and-a-half times as likely to report erectile dysfunction.

- Neither masturbation nor having had more than five sexual

SEXUAL PRACTICES IN THE UNITED STATES

Laumann, Gagnon, Michael, and Michaels reported the following findings after interviewing 3,432 Americans between the ages of 18 and 59 in 1994:

- Average age at first intercourse: 16
- Average frequency of sex: 7 times a month
- Percentage of men who have had sex with another man: 9 percent
- Percentage of women who have had sex with another woman: 4 percent
- Percentage of women who always have an orgasm during intercourse: 29 percent
- Percentage of men who had difficulties with erection in the last year: 11 percent
- Percentage of men who feel they climax too quickly: 28 percent
- Percentage of men who masturbated in the last year: 60 percent
- Percentage of women who masturbated in the last year: 60 percent

partners increases the relative risk of sexual dysfunction for either men or women.

- A history of sexually transmitted disease, moderate to high alcohol consumption, and circumcision generally do not increase the odds of experiencing sexual dysfunction.

The researchers found that roughly 10 percent of men and 20 percent of women seek medical attention for their sexual problems.

DOES TV CREATE AN IDEAL STANDARD OF SEXUALITY?

In 1989, another study, written by Dale Kunkel and colleagues for the Kaiser Family Foundation, looked at the way sexual acts are portrayed

Cast members of the TV series Friends *pose for a group photograph in London. In a study conducted for the Kaiser Family Foundation, the popular comedy was cited by name for its sexually explicit plots and dialogue.*

on popular television. The results, some critics said, indicate that "hypersexualized media"—media that is heavy with sexual incidents—contribute to unrealistic expectations about sex that leave many people feeling inadequate about their own desires and performance.

The Kaiser researchers watched 1,351 network and cable TV shows randomly selected to represent a typical broadcast week. Of the 88 TV scenes they examined that contained implied or actual sexual intercourse, the researchers found not a single reference to the dangers or potential consequences of sex, such as pregnancy or sexually transmitted diseases. This idealized world of sex, plus the amount of sex on television—85 percent of the soap operas the Kaiser researchers watched had episodes involving sexual intercourse—suggest that highly active sex lives are normal or desirable.

Sexual stereotypes may be especially harmful to women, some critics argue, because they belittle traits such as low sexual desire without determining what "normal" levels are for women. The authors of the Kaiser Family Foundation report concluded their study with a plea for television producers to broadcast a more responsible message about sexuality.

Dr. Louis J. Ignarro is a researcher at the University of California in Los Angeles. His discovery that the human body uses nitric oxide to regulate blood vessels led to the development of the anti-impotence drug Viagra. It also won him the Nobel Prize for medicine.

7

TREATING
SEXUAL DISORDERS

S exual disorders and their causes can be treated by physicians in a hospital or clinic, or by therapists in office environments. This chapter does not cover *all* disorders and their treatments, but rather presents a sample of the different approaches specialists may use in treating types of sexual disorders.

TREATING HYPOACTIVE SEXUAL DESIRE

When an individual's interest in sex is weak, or completely absent, a sexual desire disorder may be the diagnosis. Many times, when a sexual relationship is in trouble, lack of desire becomes one of the key issues between the partners. Sexual desire disorders do not involve a physical difficulty. Individuals with this disorder are capable of having sex but simply are not interested.

Physicians and therapists who treat patients for hypoactive sexual desire (HSD) recognize that there is a conditioned—or programmed—link between negative feelings and sex. This negative association must be changed or eliminated for the patient to improve. As Kaplan explains, patients with HSD "unwittingly . . . downregulate their sexual desire by accentuating the negatives and de-accentuating the positive aspects of sex." Normally, she points out, people suppress their sexual desires when the object of their desire is not appropriate—a much younger person or a relative, for example. Then, in situations where there is no conflict and desire is appropriate, lovers idealize their partners by tuning out unpleasantries and focusing on their attractive qualities. According to Kaplan, however, patients with HSD do the opposite:

> When they are faced with attractive, appropriate partners and a sexual situation that ought to be desirable, these individuals dwell on unpleasant, anxiety-provoking thoughts or "antifantasies" and focus on their partner's less attractive qualities. They also go out of their way to erect defenses against perceiving their lover's beauty, and avoid erotic fantasy as well as

effective physical stimulation; some patients with HSD even engage in countercourtship [deliberately unromantic] behaviors as an additional barrier to sexual feelings.

Patients with HSD are typically not aware they are "turning themselves off." They tend to attribute their lack of sexual desire for their partners to "poor chemistry" and often resist the idea that this could be their own doing. The specialist's job, says Kaplan, is "to help these patients see that their low desire for their partners is largely self-generated, and that they could have much more choice in the matter."

To accomplish this, physicians and therapists may use a variety of "homework assignments"—things the couple should work on privately—to help patients learn to recognize and change their antisexual thoughts, and to make them comfortable with their sexual partners. Here are some typical assignments:

- *Setting the mood*: Patients who become too tense to feel sexy may be taught relaxation techniques. Therapists may suggest taking a warm shower (alone, before approaching one's partner) or listening to relaxation tapes or music. Others may be asked to spend some time communicating to their partners their feelings and concerns about sex.

- *Courtship and dating arrangements*: Some sexually conflicted patients do unromantic things, such as being rude, insensitive, distant, or neglectful to their partners, which make a satisfying sexual relationship unlikely. A therapist may try to stop the pattern by helping couples practice being more considerate toward one another. The idea is to re-create the kind of interaction that loving couples share: cooking the partner a special dinner, taking him or her out dancing, listening sympathetically to the partner's problems, cleaning up a messy bedroom, taking showers, brushing teeth, shaving before going to bed, giving up smoking, not watching television every evening, bringing flowers, buying special presents, arranging a surprise birthday party, or dividing household money more fairly. In addition, a therapist may recommend that couples schedule events that give a high priority to intimacy and sexuality, such as "date nights" or an uninterrupted dinner together several times a week.

As a remedy for hypoactive sexual desire disorder, therapists often recommend that couples schedule events that recreate the loving feelings they experienced early in their relationships. This couple is taking the time to share a romantic breakfast.

- *Sexual skills training:* These assignments are used to correct a patient's lack of knowledge or skills about his or her partner's sexual desires. Exercises that at first involve nonsexual touching provide the couple with the opportunity to experience and learn to enjoy intimate exchanges of caresses, free of any expectations.

- *Sex education:* Some therapists take the role of teachers in helping couples learn and communicate about sex. Patients who lack desire do not know what to expect from sexual intimacy. Models of the human body may be used for couples who need information. Some patients are given sex education tapes to view at home, alone or with their partner, whichever is appropriate.

- *Dream analysis*: The interpretation of dreams often plays an important role in understanding how conflicts from childhood, painful events, or negative antisexual messages are interfering with sexuality. With the help of a therapist, patients might recognize and appreciate the meaning of recurring themes involving sex that appear in their dreams. One male patient, for example, kept dreaming that he was a knight dressed in chain mail, unable to move, in dreams where his wife was present. A therapist suggested that "chain mail" might mean a "chained male," someone who felt he was captured. In fact, the patient admitted he resented being "chained" by his wife's jealous behavior and got back at her by shutting her out emotionally and sexually.

TREATING SEXUAL AVERSION

Sexual aversion disorder presents an additional challenge to therapists. More than addressing a patient's lack of interest in sex, as in hypoactive sexual desire disorder, a therapist must try and overcome a patient's outright fear of sex. The goal is to persuade the patient that physical intimacy can be a safe experience.

During some treatments for sexual aversion disorder, patients will be instructed to participate in brief examples of intimate situations—kissing, caressing, holding hands—until fearful feelings have gone away. At first such assignments typically make patients very anxious, but eventually they become accustomed to what's happening. After patients become comfortable with one level of intimacy, they advance to the next step. Success builds on success until fear gradually gives way to feelings of confidence.

In some cases, however, it can be difficult for someone to control his or her intense fears. Patients with sexual aversion may have panic attacks, for instance, that not even the most nonthreatening intimacy assignments can overcome. In those instances, physicians may treat the panic attacks with antianxiety or panic-blocking drugs, so that patients can put their fears aside long enough to benefit from the therapy.

Occasionally, other factors outside the realm of sexuality are involved, too, that contribute to patients' lack of desire or fear—for instance,

In many parts of the world, impotence is treated with traditional remedies. This shop in Taipei, the capital of Taiwan, sells a variety of herbal medicines.

anger in the relationship, inability to trust, unresolved problems with parents, or feelings of guilt or shame about something. If a physician or therapist recognizes these problems, psychological therapy will usually be recommended before sex therapy can go ahead.

TREATING ERECTILE DYSFUNCTION

Physicians and therapists will often begin treatment of this problem by letting the patient know he is not alone in having this problem; most men are unable to generate an erection at some time in their lives. If a patient's difficulty is long-standing and causes him distress, both the physical and emotional causes of erectile dysfunction can be treated.

INTERVIEW WITH A SEX THERAPIST

The following interview is with William F. Fitzgerald, Ph.D., a specialist in marital and sexual therapy.

What is sex therapy?

The essence of psychotherapy is for someone who is experiencing some difficulty in daily functioning to talk with someone who is trained to help that person behave in a different, more fulfilling way. Sex therapy is a form of psychotherapy that involves talking but usually also includes behavioral prescriptions— homework or homeplay designed to disinhibit the individual from a sexual impediment. Ethical sex therapy never includes sexual contact between the therapist and the patient, but often includes encouragement for the patient to do sexual things in private, either alone or with a lover, that are more and more satisfying and fulfilling.

Is there a standard of what constitutes "normal" sexual behavior?

The vast majority of questions posed to sex therapists are variations on the theme "Am I normal?" We easily accept that someone five feet tall is as "normal" as someone six feet eight inches tall, but when it comes to sex, people are afraid of not being "normal." Someone who is satisfied by a sexual release once every six weeks is as "normal" as someone who achieves sexual release twice per day. There are great individual differences among people, most of which are "normal."

What is inappropriate sexual behavior?

Sexual behavior in Western civilization is considered inappropriate if it violates what someone has consented to, or is imposed on someone who is not capable of giving consent. Walking down a public street, a woman has not consented to be confronted by a nude man. Kissing, dancing, and flirting are not a promise of intercourse, and if that is demanded or taken forcibly, it is in excess of consent. Those not capable of giving consent include children, the elderly, the mentally compromised, and anyone whose judgment is distorted by alcohol or drugs. Adults with a clear mind who have some idea of the consequences of their behavior are per-

Dr. William Fitzgerald.

mitted to choose their sexual behavior, and that is considered appropriate. All else is not.

Why do women seek help for sexual problems more often than men?

First, women seek help for all kinds of problems more often than men. Men in Western civilization are encouraged to be self-sufficient and stoic, so to admit a problem is construed as a sign of weakness. Second, in the realm of sexuality, women are traditionally more passive—the passive recipients of an erect penis— where it is the man who must "perform" by achieving and maintaining an erection. Thus, men mistakenly associate sexual performance with success, and a sexual problem thus becomes a failure.

How does a person know when to seek professional help for a sexual problem?

If you believe you are operating on correct information about how things should be functioning, but they are not—and your attempts to correct that are not solving the problem—you are well advised to seek professional help before repeating the ineffective correction attempts and thereby making your ineffective behavior harder to correct.

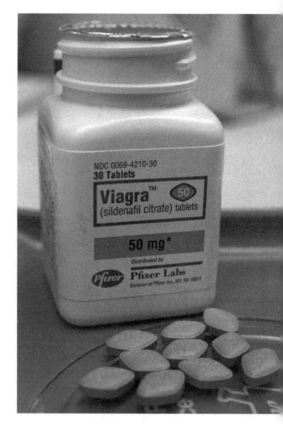

Viagra, the drug used to treat erectile dysfunction, has been immensely popular. The U.S. Food and Drug Administration approved its use in March 1998, and within two months more than 1 million men had obtained prescriptions for it.

One of the most successful treatments has been the use of homework assignments to gradually decrease anxiety about having an erection. For example, a patient who has a sexual partner may be given an assignment to give and receive regular, nonsexual massages. Gradually, the patient is told to engage in pleasurable sexual activities, until anxiety about having an erection decreases.

Physicians can offer physical treatments for erectile dysfunction, too. Viagra is the brand name of sildenafil, a medication that enables men with erectile dysfunction to have sex. This drug works by enhancing the muscle relaxant effects of nitric oxide, a chemical that the body naturally releases in response to sexual stimulation. This relaxation allows increased blood flow in to the penis, leading to an erection. It is administered one hour prior to sex, once in every 24-hour period. The patient will still need to experience physical and mental stimulation in order to have an erection. Some men who are being treated for a heart condition with nitroglycerin or who take some other medication that contains nitrates should not take Viagra.

For males who do not respond to other treatments or cannot use medications like Viagra, penile implants may be surgically added. Two types are currently available: a bendable silicon implant and an inflatable implant. However, physicians will recommend these alternatives to patients only after careful psychiatric, sexual, and urological evaluation. Follow-up studies have shown highly positive results.

TREATING PARAPHILIAS

Psychoanalysis and psychodynamic *psychotherapy* have been used in treating paraphilias. In these treatments, with the help of a specialist, a patient can learn to identify and resolve early conflicts, trauma, or humiliation that may be the root cause of the paraphilia. A second strategy, cognitive behavioral therapy, consists of using both thought- and behavior-altering assignments to change the immediate causes of the patient's paraphilia. The purpose might be to remove the individual's anxiety about who would be an appropriate sexual partner, for instance, and enable him or her to give up the paraphilic fantasies.

A variety of behavior-changing therapies have also been used to treat paraphilias. One method is called aversive conditioning. Patients will voluntarily smell bad odors while rehearsing a paraphilic fantasy in their minds, thus pairing unpleasantness with inappropriate behavior. Therapists may also guide patients through thinking about inappropriate sexual fantasies while imagining anxiety-provoking scenes. The goal is to link the paraphilia with undesirable feelings.

Additionally, drugs have been used to treat paraphilias. Triptorelin is one medication that reduces abnormal sexual thoughts and behaviors by reducing the secretion of male hormones. Other medications decrease the intensity and frequency of sexual desire and arousal. Cyproterone acetate is an experimental drug (not yet available in the United States) that not only suppresses the bizarre sexual desires, but also replaces them with an interest in relations with other consenting adults.

Studies have shown that combinations of these therapies are often the most effective in treating paraphilias. However, paraphilias are deeply rooted in a person's identity, and success rates are not high.

APPENDIX

KEY DATES IN DEFINING SEXUALITY

1843

German physician Heinrich Kaan publishes his study *Psychopathia Sexualis*, in which he argues that diseases of the mind cause "sinful" sexual behavior. Other physicians and psychiatrists also begin to use terms such as "deviation," "aberration," and "perversion." Originally, these terms referred to "false" religious beliefs; now they are used as labels for poorly defined medical concepts.

1857

The French physician B. A. Morel advances the concept of physical and mental "degeneration," which, among other things, supposedly explains sexual "misbehavior."

1864

The German lawyer Karl-Heinrich Ulrichs publishes a series of pamphlets in which he declares "man-male love" to be inborn, arguing that it is the natural, healthy expression of a "female soul in a male body." Ulrichs hopes to demonstrate the injustice of punishing sexual contact between men.

1870

The Berlin psychiatrist Carl Westphal publishes the first medical case history of same-sex erotic attraction. It concerns a woman who feels attracted to the female students in her sister's boarding school. Westphal concludes that she suffers from a psychopathological condition for which he coins a new term: "contrary sexual feeling." The "condition" of loving persons of the same sex comes to be viewed as a psychiatric illness.

1886

The Austrian psychiatrist Richard von Krafft-Ebing publishes his *Psychopathia Sexualis*, a collection of case histories documenting strange and unusual sexual practices. These supposedly point to "sexual diseases of the mind." Among other things, he introduces the concepts of "sadism" and "masochism."

1896

The English private scholar Havelock Ellis begins his *Studies in the Psychology of Sex* (last volume, 1928). Since the books cannot be published in England, they appear in the United States and in Germany.

1905

The Viennese physician Sigmund Freud publishes his "Three Essays on the Theory of Sex." In this work he describes the "normal" development of human sexuality as well as the "perversions"—behaviors that do not correspond to the norm. His theory is based on the doctrine of psychoanalysis (examination of the mind or soul).

1908

Magnus Hirschfeld edits the first *Journal of Sexology*.

1910

Hirschfeld introduces the term "transvestites," distinguishing cross-dressers from homosexuals for the first time.

1929

The English philosopher Bertrand Russell publishes his book *Marriage and Morals*, which argues for more and better sex education, the right to premarital and extramarital intercourse or "free love," and divorce on demand for childless couples. This is later used against him in the United States, where he is denied a professorship on the grounds that it would amount to establishing a "chair of indecency."

1947

Alfred C. Kinsey founds the Institute for Sex Research (today called the Kinsey Institute) at Indiana University.

The Japanese researcher Shin'ichi Asayama begins his statistical surveys of the sexual behavior of Japanese students. He repeats such surveys every five years for more than 30 years, eventually reaching a total of over 20,000 respondents.

1948

Kinsey and his collaborators Wardell B. Pomeroy and Clyde E. Martin publish their first great study, *Sexual Behavior in the Human Male*.

1953

Alfred C. Kinsey and his collaborators, Wardell B. Pomeroy, Clyde E. Martin, and Paul H. Gebhard, publish *Sexual Behavior in the Human Female*. Both "Kinsey Reports" are based on personal interviews with more than 12,000 individuals from all over the United States. Because of vehement attacks by conservative religious and political leaders, Kinsey is denied further financial support for his research.

1966

Physicians William H. Masters and his wife, Virginia Johnson, publish their study of the physiological processes during sexual activity, *Human Sexual Response*. They suggest a four-phase model of the sexual response: (1) excitement, (2) plateau, (3) orgasm, (4) resolution.

1970

Masters and Johnson publish their study of sexual dysfunctions: *Human Sexual Inadequacy.* The book becomes the basis for a new behavioral "sex therapy."

1987

Helen S. Kaplan publishes *The Illustrated Manual of Sex Therapy,* which becomes a foundation for therapy of sexual disorders from a perspective that combines the physiological and the psychological.

APPENDIX

FOR MORE INFORMATION

Advocates for Youth
1025 Vermont Avenue NW
Suite 200
Washington, DC 20005
Phone: 202-347-5700
E-mail:
  info@advocatesforyouth.org
http://www.advocatesforyouth.org

This organization provides information, education and training, and advocacy on adolescent sexual health issues.

American Association for Marriage and Family Therapy (AAMFT)
1133 15th Street NW
Suite 300
Washington, DC 20005-2710
Phone: 202-452-0109
E-mail: central@aamft.org
Fax: 202-223-2329
http://www.aamft.org

This organization is devoted to the development of professional, ethical, and educational standards for marriage and family therapists. It is also involved in therapy research and represents therapists' professional interests.

American Association of Child and Adolescent Psychiatry (AACAP)
3615 Wisconsin Avenue NW
Washington, DC 20016
Phone: 202-966-7300
http://www.aacap.org

The Association offers information about sexual orientation and sexuality issues.

American Psychiatric Association (APA)
1400 K Street NW
Washington, DC 20005
Phone: 202-682-6000
E-mail: apa@psych.org
http://www.psych.org

The Association has committees on HIV/AIDS; family violence and sexual abuse; gay, lesbian, and bisexual issues; and the diagnosis and treatment of sexual disorders.

National Coalition to Support Sexuality Education (NCSSE)
1711 Connecticut Avenue NW
Washington, DC 20009
Phone: 202-265-2405
Fax: 202-462-2340

The Coalition was begun in 1990 to promote comprehensive sexuality education for all children and youth in the United States. It now includes 112 organizations as members.

Sexuality Information and Education Council of the U.S. (SIECUS)
130 W. 42nd Street
Suite 350
New York, NY 10036-7802
Phone: 212-819-9770
Fax: 212-819-9776
E-mail: siecus@siecus.org
http://www.siecus.org

SIECUS is a national, private, non-profit advocacy organization that promotes comprehensive sexuality education and HIV/AIDS prevention education in the schools and advocates for sexual and reproductive rights.

Society for the Scientific Study of Sexuality (SSSS)
P.O. Box 208
Mount Vernon, IA 52314-0208
Phone: 319-895-8407
Fax: 319-895-6203
E-mail:
TheSociety@worldnet.att.net
http://www.sssswr.org

SSSS is an interdisciplinary, international organization for sexuality researchers, clinicians, educators, and other professionals in related fields.

APPENDIX

BIBLIOGRAPHY

Abel, G. G., and C. A. Osborn. "Pedophilia." In G. O. Gabbard, ed., *Treatments of Psychiatric Disorders*, 2nd edition, volumes 1–2. Washington, DC: American Psychiatric Press, 1995.

American Psychiatric Association. *Diagnostic and Statistical Manual of Mental Disorders.* 4th edition. Washington, DC: American Psychiatric Press, 1994.

Blank, Jonah. "Heather Locklear, Would-Be Role Model." *U.S. News & World Report* 126 (February 22, 1999): 59.

Brown, George R. "Transvestitism." In G. O. Gabbard, ed., *Treatments of Psychiatric Disorders*, 2nd edition, volumes 1–2. Washington, DC: American Psychiatric Press, 1995.

Bureau of Justice Statistics, Criminal Offenders Statistics. *Sex Offenders.* Online at http://www.ojp.usdoj.gov/bjs/crimoff.htm#sex [accessed December 31, 1999]

Ernst, Morris L., and David Loth. *American Sexual Behavior and the Kinsey Report.* New York: Greystone Press, 1948.

Feldman, Miriam Karmel. "The Pharma Sutra." *Utne Reader* (July–August 1999): 16.

Foa, E. B., D. S. Riggs, and B. S. Gershuny. "Arousal, Numbing, and Intrusion." *American Journal of Psychiatry* 152 (1995): 116.

Hales, Robert E., Stuart C. Yudofsky, and John A. Talbott. *The American Psychiatric Press Textbook of Psychiatry.* Washington, DC: American Psychiatric Press, 1999.

Herbert, Wray. "Not Tonight, Dear." *U.S. News & World Report* 126 (February 22, 1999): 57.

Howells, Kevin, ed. *The Psychology of Sexual Diversity.* New York: Blackwell, 1994.

Institute for Sex Research. *Sexual Behavior in the Human Female.* Philadelphia: W. B. Saunders, 1953.

Kaplan, Helen Singer. "Hypoactive Sexual Desire and Sexual Aversion." In G. O. Gabbard, ed., *Treatments of Psychiatric Disorders*, 2nd edition, volumes 1–2. Washington, DC: American Psychiatric Press, 1995.

Kaplan, Helen Singer. *The Sexual Desire Disorders: Dysfunctional Regulation of Sexual Disorders*. Levittown, PA: Brunner/Mazel, 1995.

Kinsey, Alfred C., Wardell B. Pomeroy, and Clyde E. Martin. *Sexual Behavior in the Human Male*. Philadelphia: W. B. Saunders, 1948.

Kunkel, Dale, Kirstie M. Cope, Wendy Jo Maynard Farinola, Erica Biely, Emma Rollin, and Edward Donnerstein. *Sex on TV: Content and Context. A Biennial Report to the Henry J. Kaiser Family Foundation*. February 1989. Online at http://www. kff.org/content/archive/1457/sex_rp.pdf. [Accessed May 23, 2000]

Langevin, Ron, ed. *Erotic Preference, Gender Identity, and Aggression in Men: New Research Studies*. Hillsdale, NJ: Erlbaum, 1995.

Laumann, Edward O., John H. Gagnon, Robert T. Michael, and S. Michaels. *The Social Organization of Sexuality: Sexual Practices in the United States*. Chicago: University of Chicago Press, 1994.

Leland, John. "Bad News in the Bedroom." *Newsweek* 133 (February 22, 1999): 47.

Masters, William H., and Virginia E. Johnson. *Human Sexual Inadequacy*. Boston: Little. Brown, 1970.

Masters, William H., and Virginia E. Johnson. *Human Sexual Response*. Boston: Little, Brown, 1966

Michael, Robert. *Sex in America: A Definitive Survey*. New York: Little, Brown, 1994.

Moir, Anne, and David Jessel. *Brain Sex: The Real Difference Between Men and Women*. New York: Carol Publishing Group, 1991.

Smith, Tom W. *American Sexual Behavior: Trends, Socio-Demographic Differences, and Risk Behavior*. National Opinion Research Center, University of Chicago, 1998. Online at http://www.norc.uchicago.edu/online/sex.pdf. [Accessed May 24, 2000]

APPENDIX

FURTHER READING

Ayer, Eleanor H. *It's Okay to Say No: Choosing Sexual Abstinence*. New York: Rosen, 1997.

Basso, Michael J. *The Underground Guide to Teenage Sexuality*. Minneapolis: Fairview Press, 1991.

Bell, Ruth. *Changing Bodies, Changing Lives: A Book for Teens on Sex and Relationships*. New York: Times Books, 1998.

Heron, Ann. *Two Teenagers in 20: Writings by Gay and Lesbian Youth*. Los Angeles: Alyson Publications, 1995.

Madara, Lynda. *My Body, My Self, for Boys*. New York: Newmarket Press, 1995.

Madara, Lynda. *My Body, My Self, for Girls*. New York: Newmarket Press, 1993.

Moe, Barbara A. *Everything You Need to Know About Sexual Abstinence*. New York: Rosen, 1996.

Slap, Gail B., and Martha M. Jabloe. *Sexuality and Reproduction. Teenage Health Care: The First Comprehensive Family Guide for the Preteen to Young Adult Years*. New York: Pocket Books, 1994.

Stewart, Felicia, Felicia Guest, Gary Stewart, and Robert Hatcher. *Understanding Your Body*. New York: Bantam, 1987.

Whipple, Beverly, and Gina Ogden. *Safe Encounters: How Women Can Say Yes to Pleasure and No to Unsafe Sex*. New York: McGraw-Hill, 1989.

APPENDIX

GLOSSARY

Conditioning: a learning process by which an act or response becomes associated with a particular stimulus.

Ejaculate: to expel semen through the penis to the outside of the body.

Endogamy: marriage within a specific group, as required by custom or law.

Epilepsy: a physical disorder that involves disturbed electrical rhythms in the central nervous system.

Erection: the process whereby the penis becomes engorged with blood, causing it to increase in size.

Exhibitionism: the act of exposing one's genitals to an unwilling observer.

Exogamy: marriage outside of a specific group, as required by custom or law.

Fetish: an inanimate object or part of the body that provides sexual arousal.

Frotteurism: the act of deriving sexual pleasure from rubbing against someone in a public place.

Gender: the psychosocial aspects of being male or female.

Genitalia: the external organs of the reproductive system.

Gynecologist: a physician who cares for the female reproductive system and breasts.

Hormones: chemicals formed by the body that stimulate or suppress cell and tissue activity.

Impotent: unable to sustain an erection.

Imprinting: a rapid learning process that takes place early in an individual's life.

Incest: sexual contact between two people who belong to same immediate family.

Limbic system: a system in the brain that influences sexual behavior, as well as other emotions and motivations.

Masturbation: self-stimulation of one's genitals for sexual pleasure.

Orgasm: the climax or peak point of sexual excitement.

Prostitution: the exchange of sexual services for money.

Psychotherapy: a verbal interaction between a client and therapist designed to improve a person's adjustment to life.

Puberty: the stage of life between childhood and adulthood during which the reproductive organs mature.

Rape: sexual intercourse that occurs without consent as the result of actual or threatened force.

Sexual abuse: the destructive use of another human being as a sexual object.

Transvestitism: the act of deriving contentment or sexual arousal from the act of wearing clothing of the opposite sex.

Vagina: the muscular canal between the uterus and the outside of a woman's body.

Voyeurism: the act of obtaining sexual gratification by observing people, without their consent, who are undressed or engaged in sexual interaction.

APPENDIX

INDEX

APPENDIX

PICTURE CREDITS

page

8: © VCG/FPG International LLC
10: © Will and Deni McIntyre,
Science Source/Photo Researchers
12: © VCG/FPG International LLC
16: © Eric O'Connell/FPG
International LLC
18: © VCG/FPG International LLC
20: © Katrina Thomas/Photo
Researchers
22: AP/Wide World Photos
25: Archive Photos
26: AP/Wide World Photos
27: AP/Wide World Photos
29: © Margaret Miller/Photo
Researchers
30: © Blair Seitz, Science
Source/Photo Researchers
33 © Richard Nowitz, Science
Source/Photo Researchers
35: © Ken Cavanagh, Science
Source/Photo Researchers
36: © VCG/FPG International LLC

38: AP/Wide World Photos
41: Phil Schermeister/Corbis
44: © Barbara Rios/Photo Researchers
46: © M. B. Duda/Photo Researchers
50: AP/Wide World Photos
52: © Margaret Miller, Science
Source/Photo Researchers
55: © Corbis
56: © VCG/FPG International LLC
58: © Michael Krasowitz/FPG
International LLC
61: © VCG/FPG International LLC
63: AP/Wide World Photos
64: AP/Wide World Photos
67: © Richard Price/FPG
International LLC
69: AP/Wide World Photos
71: Courtesy Dr. William Fitzgerald
72: AP/Wide World Photos

Senior Consulting Editor Carol C. Nadelson, M.D., is president and chief executive officer of the American Psychiatric Press, Inc., staff physician at Cambridge Hospital, and Clinical Professor of Psychiatry at Harvard Medical School. In addition to her work with the American Psychiatric Association, which she served as vice president in 1981–83 and president in 1985–86, Dr. Nadelson has been actively involved in other major psychiatric organizations, including the Group for the Advancement of Psychiatry, the American College of Psychiatrists, the Association for Academic Psychiatry, the American Association of Directors of Psychiatric Residency Training Programs, the American Psychosomatic Society, and the American College of Mental Health Administrators. In addition, she has been a consultant to the Psychiatric Education Branch of the National Institute of Mental Health and has served on the editorial boards of several journals. Doctor Nadelson has received many awards, including the Gold Medal Award for significant and ongoing contributions in the field of psychiatry, the Elizabeth Blackwell Award for contributions to the causes of women in medicine, and the Distinguished Service Award from the American College of Psychiatrists for outstanding achievements and leadership in the field of psychiatry.

Consulting Editor Claire E. Reinburg, M.A., is editorial director of the American Psychiatric Press, Inc., which publishes about 60 new books and six journals a year. She is a graduate of Georgetown University in Washington, D.C., where she earned bachelor of arts and master of arts degrees in English. She is a member of the Council of Biology Editors, the Women's National Book Association, the Society for Scholarly Publishing, and Washington Book Publishers.

Charles Shields was formerly the chairman of the guidance department at Homewood-Flossmoor High School in Flossmoor, Illinois. He currently writes full-time from his home in Homewood, Illinois, where he lives with his wife, Guadalupe, an elementary school principal.